My Novel Idea

_____

_____

My working title.

This Book
Belongs To

_____

_____

_____

Please Return With Care

Barbara Appleby Books

My Novel Idea

By

Barbara Appleby

I am not going to tell you how to write a novel there
are too many good books out there.
This is to help you get organized and and
to get that book down on
paper.

To be the first to know what books
we have out please sign up for our
newsletter at:

barbaraappleby.weebly.com

Delight thyself in the Lord: and he will give thee the desires of thine heart.
Psalms 37:4 (KJV)

Barbara Appleby Books

Directions

You have this idea for a book. It could be a best seller. But how do you get it down on paper and organized. Yes I know you have it on napkins, the back of the grocery bill and down the side of your to do list. But that's not going to work is it? Now go gather them together and let's make sense of this shall we. Ok,have you got them.?

Let's get out the stick notes and pens. One idea on each sticky note. Then put them on the Sticky Notes of Ideas pages.

Now on to the Act pages. You know, what happens in what order. After that the Chapters pages and fill it in some more. Wow! Looks like you have an outline!

You can do this you know. You can take this book with you and write on your Idea for your book everywhere you go. Everything in one place.

I know you will love it. I do!

There is 40 Chapter pages and 20 Character pages to fill in for your idea.

Supplies

Stick Notes
Ink Pens
Pencils
Permanent Marker

STICKY NOTES OF IDEAS

Place
Stick Notes
here.

STICKY NOTES OF IDEAS

Notes

Notes

Acts

Act 1.

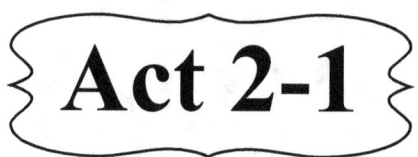

Act 2-1

Act 2-2

Act 3.

Chapter Idea Pages

What happens in each chapter?
Remember no one will see this but you.

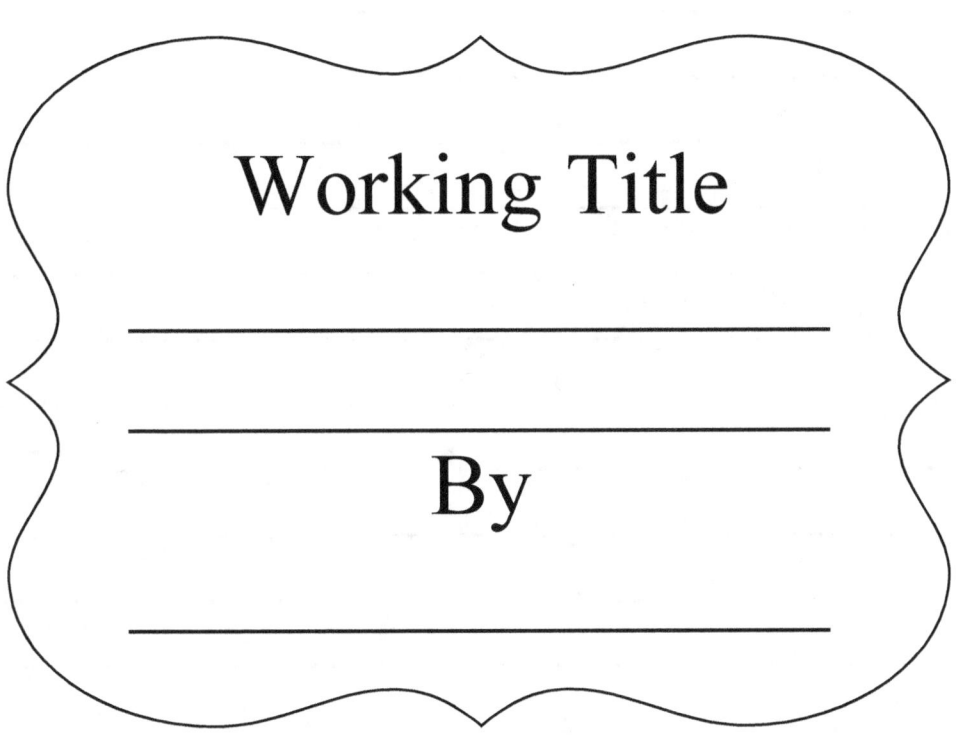

Working Title

_____

_____

By

_____

Notes

Notes

Scenes and Ideas for Chapter _____

Novel Idea

Chapter:	Setting:	Day or Night Time:_____
Main Characters in the scene: _____ _____ _____ _____ _____ **Other Characters in the scene:** _____ _____ _____ _____ _____ What event must this come before or after: _____	Main action in this scene: Main Conflict: This scene is provoked by	EFFECTS: Sound_____ Light_____ Smell_____ Taste_____ Touch_____ Sight_____ Main Effects:

What Happened

Beginning_____

_____

_____

_____

Middle_____

_____

_____

_____

End_____

_____

_____

_____

Scenes and Ideas for Chapter _____

Novel Idea

Chapter:	Setting:	Day or Night Time:_____
Main Characters in the scene: _____ _____ _____ _____ _____ **Other Characters in the scene:** _____ _____ _____ _____ _____ **What event must this come before or after:** _____ _____	Main action in this scene: Main Conflict: This scene is provoked by	EFFECTS: Sound_____ Light_____ Smell_____ Taste_____ Touch_____ Sight_____ Main Effects:

What Happened

Beginning_____

_____

_____

_____

Middle_____

_____

_____

_____

End_____

_____

_____

Scenes and Ideas for Chapter _____

Novel Idea

Chapter:	Setting:	Day or Night Time:_____
Main Characters in the scene: _____ _____ _____ _____ _____ **Other Characters in the scene:** _____ _____ _____ _____ **What event must this come before or after:** _____	Main action in this scene: Main Conflict: This scene is provoked by	EFFECTS: Sound_____ Light_____ Smell_____ Taste_____ Touch_____ Sight_____ Main Effects:

What Happened

Beginning_____

_____

_____

_____

Middle_____

_____

_____

_____

End_____

_____

_____

_____

Scenes and Ideas for Chapter _____

Novel Idea

Chapter:	Setting:	Day or Night Time:_____
Main Characters in the scene: _____ _____ _____ _____ **Other Characters in the scene:** _____ _____ _____ _____ What event must this come before or after: _____	Main action in this scene: Main Conflict: This scene is provoked by	EFFECTS: Sound_____ Light_____ Smell_____ Taste_____ Touch_____ Sight_____ Main Effects:

What Happened

Beginning_____

_____

_____

_____

Middle_____

_____

_____

_____

End_____

_____

_____

Scenes and Ideas for Chapter _____

Novel Idea

Chapter:	Setting:	Day or Night Time:_____
Main Characters in the scene: _____ _____ _____ _____ _____ Other Characters in the scene: _____ _____ _____ _____ _____ What event must this come before or after: _____	Main action in this scene: Main Conflict: This scene is provoked by	EFFECTS: Sound_____ Light_____ Smell_____ Taste_____ Touch_____ Sight_____ Main Effects:

What Happened

Beginning_____

_____

_____

_____

Middle_____

_____

_____

_____

End_____

_____

_____

_____

Scenes and Ideas for Chapter _____

Novel Idea

Chapter:	Setting:	Day or Night Time:_____
Main Characters in the scene: _____ _____ _____ _____ **Other Characters in the scene:** _____ _____ _____ _____ _____ **What event must this come before or after:** _____	**Main action in this scene:** **Main Conflict:** **This scene is provoked by**	**EFFECTS:** Sound_____ Light_____ Smell_____ Taste_____ Touch_____ Sight_____ **Main Effects:**

What Happened

Beginning_____

_____

_____

_____

Middle_____

_____

_____

_____

End_____

_____

_____

_____

Scenes and Ideas for Chapter _____

Novel Idea

Chapter:	Setting:	Day or Night Time:_____
Main Characters in the scene: _____ _____ _____ _____ Other Characters in the scene: _____ _____ _____ _____ _____ What event must this come before or after: _____	Main action in this scene: Main Conflict: This scene is provoked by	EFFECTS: Sound_____ Light_____ Smell_____ Taste_____ Touch_____ Sight_____ Main Effects:

What Happened

Beginning_____

_____

_____

_____

Middle_____

_____

_____

_____

End_____

_____

_____

_____

Scenes and Ideas for Chapter _____

Novel Idea

Chapter:	Setting:	Day or Night Time:_____
Main Characters in the scene: _____ _____ _____ _____ Other Characters in the scene: _____ _____ _____ _____ _____ What event must this come before or after: _____	Main action in this scene: Main Conflict: This scene is provoked by	EFFECTS: Sound_____ Light_____ Smell_____ Taste_____ Touch_____ Sight_____ Main Effects:

What Happened

Beginning_____

_____

_____

_____

Middle_____

_____

_____

_____

End_____

_____

_____

_____

Scenes and Ideas for Chapter _____

Novel Idea

Chapter:	Setting:	Day or Night Time:_____
Main Characters in the scene: _____ _____ _____ _____	**Main action in this scene:**	**EFFECTS:** Sound_____ Light_____ Smell_____ Taste_____ Touch_____ Sight_____
Other Characters in the scene: _____ _____ _____ _____ _____	**Main Conflict:** **This scene is provoked by**	**Main Effects:**
What event must this come before or after: _____		

What Happened

Beginning_____

_____

_____

_____

Middle_____

_____

_____

_____

End_____

_____

_____

_____

Scenes and Ideas for Chapter _____

Novel Idea

Chapter:	Setting:	Day or Night Time:_____
Main Characters in the scene: _____ _____ _____ _____ **Other Characters in the scene:** _____ _____ _____ _____ **What event must this come before or after:** _____	Main action in this scene: Main Conflict: This scene is provoked by	EFFECTS: Sound_____ Light_____ Smell_____ Taste_____ Touch_____ Sight_____ Main Effects:

What Happened

Beginning_____

_____

_____

_____

Middle_____

_____

_____

_____

End_____

_____

_____

Scenes and Ideas for Chapter _____

Novel Idea

Chapter:	Setting:	Day or Night Time:_____
Main Characters in the scene: _____ _____ _____ _____ **Other Characters in the scene:** _____ _____ _____ _____ _____ **What event must this come before or after:** _____	**Main action in this scene:** **Main Conflict:** **This scene is provoked by**	**EFFECTS:** Sound_____ Light_____ Smell_____ Taste_____ Touch_____ Sight_____ **Main Effects:**

What Happened

Beginning_____

_____

_____

_____

Middle_____

_____

_____

End_____

_____

_____

Scenes and Ideas for Chapter _____

Novel Idea

Chapter:	Setting:	Day or Night Time:_____
Main Characters in the scene: _____ _____ _____ _____ **Other Characters in the scene:** _____ _____ _____ _____ _____ **What event must this come before or after:** _____	**Main action in this scene:** **Main Conflict:** **This scene is provoked by**	**EFFECTS:** Sound_____ Light_____ Smell_____ Taste_____ Touch_____ Sight_____ Main Effects:

What Happened

Beginning_____

_____

_____

_____

Middle_____

_____

_____

_____

End_____

_____

_____

Scenes and Ideas for Chapter _____

Novel Idea

Chapter:	Setting:	Day or Night Time:_____
Main Characters in the scene: _____ _____ _____ _____ **Other Characters in the scene:** _____ _____ _____ _____ _____ **What event must this come before or after:** _____	**Main action in this scene:** **Main Conflict:** **This scene is provoked by**	**EFFECTS:** Sound_____ Light_____ Smell_____ Taste_____ Touch_____ Sight_____ **Main Effects:**

What Happened

Beginning_____

_____

_____

_____

Middle_____

_____

_____

End_____

_____

_____

Scenes and Ideas for Chapter _____

Novel Idea

Chapter:	Setting:	Day or Night Time:_____
Main Characters in the scene: _____ _____ _____ _____ **Other Characters in the scene:** _____ _____ _____ _____ **What event must this come before or after:** _____	**Main action in this scene:** **Main Conflict:** **This scene is provoked by**	**EFFECTS:** Sound_____ Light_____ Smell_____ Taste_____ Touch_____ Sight_____ **Main Effects:**

What Happened

Beginning_____

_____

_____

_____

Middle_____

_____

_____

End_____

_____

_____

Scenes and Ideas for Chapter _____

Novel Idea

Chapter:	Setting:	Day or Night Time:_____
Main Characters in the scene: _____ _____ _____ _____ **Other Characters in the scene:** _____ _____ _____ _____ _____ **What event must this come before or after:** _____	Main action in this scene: Main Conflict: This scene is provoked by	EFFECTS: Sound_____ Light_____ Smell_____ Taste_____ Touch_____ Sight_____ Main Effects:

What Happened

Beginning_____

_____

_____

_____

Middle_____

_____

_____

End_____

_____

_____

_____

Scenes and Ideas for Chapter _____

Novel Idea

Chapter:	Setting:	Day or Night Time:_____
Main Characters in the scene: _____ _____ _____ _____ **Other Characters in the scene:** _____ _____ _____ _____ **What event must this come before or after:** _____	Main action in this scene: Main Conflict: This scene is provoked by	EFFECTS: Sound_____ Light_____ Smell_____ Taste_____ Touch_____ Sight_____ Main Effects:

What Happened

Beginning_____

_____

_____

_____

Middle_____

_____

_____

_____

End_____

_____

_____

Scenes and Ideas for Chapter _____

Novel Idea

Chapter:	Setting:	Day or Night Time:_____
Main Characters in the scene: _____ _____ _____ _____ _____ **Other Characters in the scene:** _____ _____ _____ _____ _____ **What event must this come before or after:** _____	Main action in this scene: Main Conflict: This scene is provoked by	EFFECTS: Sound_____ Light_____ Smell_____ Taste_____ Touch_____ Sight_____ Main Effects:

What Happened

Beginning_____

_____

_____

_____

Middle_____

_____

_____

_____

End_____

_____

_____

Scenes and Ideas for Chapter _____

Novel Idea

Chapter:	Setting:	Day or Night Time:_____
Main Characters in the scene: _____ _____ _____ _____ **Other Characters in the scene:** _____ _____ _____ _____ _____ **What event must this come before or after:** _____	**Main action in this scene:** **Main Conflict:** **This scene is provoked by**	**EFFECTS:** Sound_____ Light_____ Smell_____ Taste_____ Touch_____ Sight_____ **Main Effects:**

What Happened

Beginning_____

_____

_____

_____

Middle_____

_____

_____

_____

End_____

_____

_____

_____

Scenes and Ideas for Chapter _____

Novel Idea

Chapter:	Setting:	Day or Night Time:_____
Main Characters in the scene: _____ _____ _____ _____ Other Characters in the scene: _____ _____ _____ _____ _____ What event must this come before or after: _____	Main action in this scene: Main Conflict: This scene is provoked by	EFFECTS: Sound_____ Light_____ Smell_____ Taste_____ Touch_____ Sight_____ Main Effects:

What Happened

Beginning_____

_____

_____

_____

Middle_____

_____

_____

_____

End_____

_____

_____

Scenes and Ideas for Chapter _____

Novel Idea

Chapter:	Setting:	Day or Night Time:_____
Main Characters in the scene: _____ _____ _____ _____ **Other Characters in the scene:** _____ _____ _____ _____ _____ **What event must this come before or after:** _____	**Main action in this scene:** **Main Conflict:** **This scene is provoked by**	**EFFECTS:** Sound_____ Light_____ Smell_____ Taste_____ Touch_____ Sight_____ **Main Effects:**

What Happened

Beginning_____

_____

_____

_____

Middle_____

_____

_____

_____

End_____

_____

_____

Scenes and Ideas for Chapter _____

Novel Idea

Chapter:	Setting:	Day or Night Time:_____
Main Characters in the scene: _____ _____ _____ _____ Other Characters in the scene: _____ _____ _____ _____ What event must this come before or after: _____	Main action in this scene: Main Conflict: This scene is provoked by	EFFECTS: Sound_____ Light_____ Smell_____ Taste_____ Touch_____ Sight_____ Main Effects:

What Happened

Beginning_____

_____

_____

_____

Middle_____

_____

_____

_____

End_____

_____

_____

_____

Scenes and Ideas for Chapter _____

Novel Idea

Chapter:	Setting:	Day or Night Time:_____
Main Characters in the scene: _____ _____ _____ _____ **Other Characters in the scene:** _____ _____ _____ _____ **What event must this come before or after:** _____	**Main action in this scene:** **Main Conflict:** **This scene is provoked by**	**EFFECTS:** Sound_____ Light_____ Smell_____ Taste_____ Touch_____ Sight_____ **Main Effects:**

What Happened

Beginning_____

_____

_____

_____

Middle_____

_____

_____

_____

End_____

_____

_____

Scenes and Ideas for Chapter _____

Novel Idea

Chapter:	Setting:	Day or Night Time:_____
Main Characters in the scene: _____ _____ _____ _____ **Other Characters in the scene:** _____ _____ _____ _____ _____ **What event must this come before or after:** _____	**Main action in this scene:** **Main Conflict:** **This scene is provoked by**	**EFFECTS:** Sound_____ Light_____ Smell_____ Taste_____ Touch_____ Sight_____ **Main Effects:**

What Happened

Beginning_____

_____

_____

_____

Middle_____

_____

_____

_____

End_____

_____

_____

_____

Scenes and Ideas for Chapter _____

Novel Idea

Chapter:	Setting:	Day or Night Time:_____
Main Characters in the scene: _____ _____ _____ _____ **Other Characters in the scene:** _____ _____ _____ _____ _____ **What event must this come before or after:** _____	**Main action in this scene:** **Main Conflict:** **This scene is provoked by**	**EFFECTS:** Sound_____ Light_____ Smell_____ Taste_____ Touch_____ Sight_____ **Main Effects:**

What Happened

Beginning_____

_____

_____

_____

Middle_____

_____

_____

_____

End_____

_____

_____

Scenes and Ideas for Chapter _____

Novel Idea

Chapter:	Setting:	Day or Night Time:_____
Main Characters in the scene: _____ _____ _____ _____ **Other Characters in the scene:** _____ _____ _____ _____ _____ **What event must this come before or after:** _____	Main action in this scene: Main Conflict: This scene is provoked by	EFFECTS: Sound_____ Light_____ Smell_____ Taste_____ Touch_____ Sight_____ Main Effects:

What Happened

Beginning_____

_____

_____

_____

Middle_____

_____

_____

_____

End_____

_____

_____

Scenes and Ideas for Chapter _____

Novel Idea

Chapter:	Setting:	Day or Night Time:_____
Main Characters in the scene: _____ _____ _____ _____ _____ **Other Characters in the scene:** _____ _____ _____ _____ **What event must this come before or after:** _____	Main action in this scene: Main Conflict: This scene is provoked by	EFFECTS: Sound_____ Light_____ Smell_____ Taste_____ Touch_____ Sight_____ Main Effects:

What Happened

Beginning_____

_____

_____

_____

Middle_____

_____

_____

_____

End_____

_____

_____

_____

Scenes and Ideas for Chapter _____

Novel Idea

Chapter:	Setting:	Day or Night Time:_____
Main Characters in the scene: _____ _____ _____ _____ **Other Characters in the scene:** _____ _____ _____ _____ **What event must this come before or after:** _____	**Main action in this scene:** **Main Conflict:** **This scene is provoked by**	EFFECTS: Sound_____ Light_____ Smell_____ Taste_____ Touch_____ Sight_____ Main Effects:

What Happened

Beginning_____

_____

_____

_____

Middle_____

_____

_____

_____

End_____

_____

_____

_____

Scenes and Ideas for Chapter _____

Novel Idea

Chapter:	Setting:	Day or Night Time:_____
Main Characters in the scene: _____ _____ _____ _____ **Other Characters in the scene:** _____ _____ _____ _____ _____ What event must this come before or after: _____	**Main action in this scene:** **Main Conflict:** **This scene is provoked by**	EFFECTS: Sound_____ Light_____ Smell_____ Taste_____ Touch_____ Sight_____ Main Effects:

What Happened

Beginning_____

_____

_____

_____

Middle_____

_____

_____

_____

End_____

_____

_____

_____

Scenes and Ideas for Chapter _____

Novel Idea

Chapter:	Setting:	Day or Night Time:_____
Main Characters in the scene: _____ _____ _____ _____ **Other Characters in the scene:** _____ _____ _____ _____ **What event must this come before or after:** _____	**Main action in this scene:** **Main Conflict:** **This scene is provoked by**	**EFFECTS:** Sound_____ Light_____ Smell_____ Taste_____ Touch_____ Sight_____ **Main Effects:**

What Happened

Beginning_____

_____

_____

_____

Middle_____

_____

_____

_____

End_____

_____

_____

_____

Scenes and Ideas for Chapter _____

Novel Idea

Chapter:	Setting:	Day or Night Time:_____
Main Characters in the scene: _____ _____ _____ _____ **Other Characters in the scene:** _____ _____ _____ _____ _____ **What event must this come before or after:** _____	**Main action in this scene:** **Main Conflict:** **This scene is provoked by**	**EFFECTS:** Sound_____ Light_____ Smell_____ Taste_____ Touch_____ Sight_____ **Main Effects:**

What Happened

Beginning_____

_____

_____

_____

Middle_____

_____

_____

_____

End_____

_____

_____

Scenes and Ideas for Chapter _____

Novel Idea

Chapter:	Setting:	Day or Night Time:_____
Main Characters in the scene: _____ _____ _____ _____ _____ **Other Characters in the scene:** _____ _____ _____ _____ _____ **What event must this come before or after:** _____	Main action in this scene: Main Conflict: This scene is provoked by	EFFECTS: Sound_____ Light_____ Smell_____ Taste_____ Touch_____ Sight_____ Main Effects:

What Happened

Beginning_____

_____

_____

_____

Middle_____

_____

_____

_____

End_____

_____

_____

Scenes and Ideas for Chapter _____

Novel Idea

Chapter:	Setting:	Day or Night Time:_____
Main Characters in the scene: _____ _____ _____ _____ **Other Characters in the scene:** _____ _____ _____ _____ _____ **What event must this come before or after:** _____	**Main action in this scene:** **Main Conflict:** **This scene is provoked by**	**EFFECTS:** Sound_____ Light_____ Smell_____ Taste_____ Touch_____ Sight_____ **Main Effects:**

What Happened

Beginning_____

_____

_____

_____

Middle_____

_____

_____

End_____

_____

_____

Scenes and Ideas for Chapter _____

Novel Idea

Chapter:	Setting:	Day or Night Time:_____
Main Characters in the scene: _____ _____ _____ _____ Other Characters in the scene: _____ _____ _____ _____ _____ What event must this come before or after: _____	Main action in this scene: Main Conflict: This scene is provoked by	EFFECTS: Sound_____ Light_____ Smell_____ Taste_____ Touch_____ Sight_____ Main Effects:

What Happened

Beginning_____

_____

_____

_____

Middle_____

_____

_____

_____

End_____

_____

_____

Scenes and Ideas for Chapter _____

Novel Idea

Chapter:	Setting:	Day or Night Time:_____
Main Characters in the scene: _____ _____ _____ _____ **Other Characters in the scene:** _____ _____ _____ _____ **What event must this come before or after:** _____	**Main action in this scene:** **Main Conflict:** **This scene is provoked by**	**EFFECTS:** Sound_____ Light_____ Smell_____ Taste_____ Touch_____ Sight_____ **Main Effects:**

What Happened

Beginning_____

_____

_____

_____

Middle_____

_____

_____

_____

End_____

_____

_____

Scenes and Ideas for Chapter _____

Novel Idea

Chapter:	Setting:	Day or Night Time:_____
Main Characters in the scene: _____ _____ _____ _____ Other Characters in the scene: _____ _____ _____ _____ _____ What event must this come before or after: _____	Main action in this scene: Main Conflict: This scene is provoked by	EFFECTS: Sound_____ Light_____ Smell_____ Taste_____ Touch_____ Sight_____ Main Effects:

What Happened

Beginning_____

_____

_____

_____

Middle_____

_____

_____

_____

End_____

_____

_____

Scenes and Ideas for Chapter _____

Novel Idea

Chapter:	Setting:	Day or Night Time:_____
Main Characters in the scene: _____ _____ _____ _____ **Other Characters in the scene:** _____ _____ _____ _____ **What event must this come before or after:** _____	**Main action in this scene:** **Main Conflict:** **This scene is provoked by**	**EFFECTS:** Sound_____ Light_____ Smell_____ Taste_____ Touch_____ Sight_____ **Main Effects:**

What Happened

Beginning_____

_____

_____

_____

Middle_____

_____

_____

_____

End_____

_____

_____

Scenes and Ideas for Chapter _____

Novel Idea

Chapter:	Setting:	Day or Night Time:_____
Main Characters in the scene: _____ _____ _____ _____ Other Characters in the scene: _____ _____ _____ _____ What event must this come before or after: _____	Main action in this scene: Main Conflict: This scene is provoked by	EFFECTS: Sound_____ Light_____ Smell_____ Taste_____ Touch_____ Sight_____ Main Effects:

What Happened

Beginning_____

_____

_____

_____

Middle_____

_____

_____

_____

End_____

_____

_____

Scenes and Ideas for Chapter _____

Novel Idea

Chapter:	Setting:	Day or Night Time:_____
Main Characters in the scene: _____ _____ _____ _____ **Other Characters in the scene:** _____ _____ _____ _____ **What event must this come before or after:** _____	**Main action in this scene:** **Main Conflict:** **This scene is provoked by**	**EFFECTS:** Sound_____ Light_____ Smell_____ Taste_____ Touch_____ Sight_____ **Main Effects:**

What Happened

Beginning_____

_____

_____

_____

Middle_____

_____

_____

_____

End_____

_____

_____

Scenes and Ideas for Chapter _____

Novel Idea

Chapter:	Setting:	Day or Night Time:_____
Main Characters in the scene: _____ _____ _____ _____ _____ Other Characters in the scene: _____ _____ _____ _____ _____ What event must this come before or after: _____	Main action in this scene: Main Conflict: This scene is provoked by	EFFECTS: Sound_____ Light_____ Smell_____ Taste_____ Touch_____ Sight_____ Main Effects:

What Happened

Beginning_____

_____

_____

_____

Middle_____

_____

_____

_____

End_____

_____

_____

Scenes and Ideas for Chapter _____

Novel Idea

Chapter:	Setting:	Day or Night Time:_____
Main Characters in the scene: _____ _____ _____ _____ _____ **Other Characters in the scene:** _____ _____ _____ _____ _____ **What event must this come before or after:** _____	Main action in this scene: Main Conflict: This scene is provoked by	EFFECTS: Sound_____ Light_____ Smell_____ Taste_____ Touch_____ Sight_____ Main Effects:

What Happened

Beginning_____

_____

_____

_____

Middle_____

_____

_____

_____

End_____

_____

_____

Getting to Know Your Characters

_____

_____

_____

_____

_____

_____

_____

_____

_____

_____

_____

_____

_____

_____

_____

_____

_____

_____

Notes

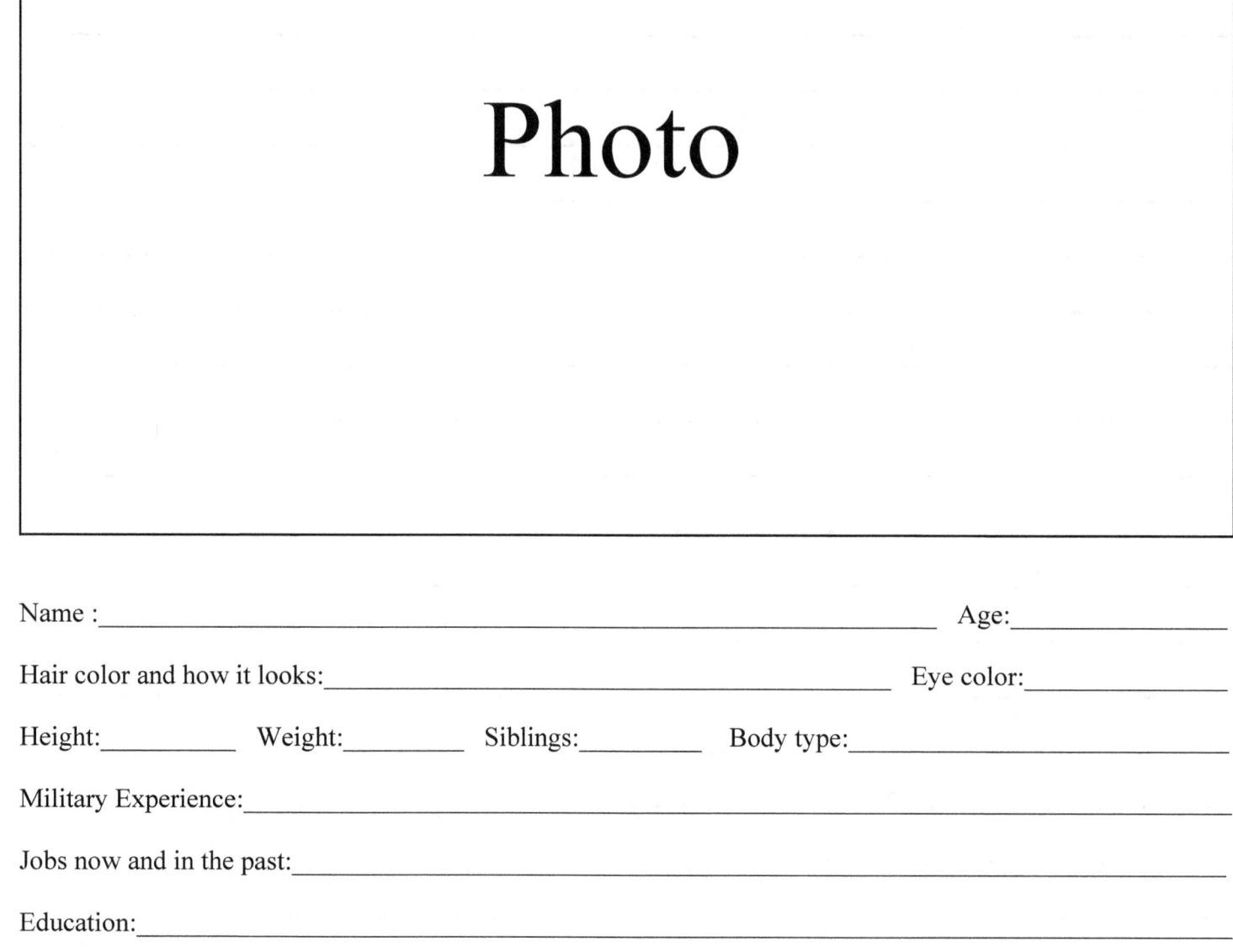

Photo

Name :_____ Age:_____

Hair color and how it looks:_____ Eye color:_____

Height:_____ Weight:_____ Siblings:_____ Body type:_____

Military Experience:_____

Jobs now and in the past:_____

Education:_____

Assets:_____

Strengths:_____

Weakness:_____

What does your character want out of life?_____

_____

What are your characters secrets?_____

_____

Does your character have a pet?_____

You get the idea. Have a conversion with your character and write it down.

Notes

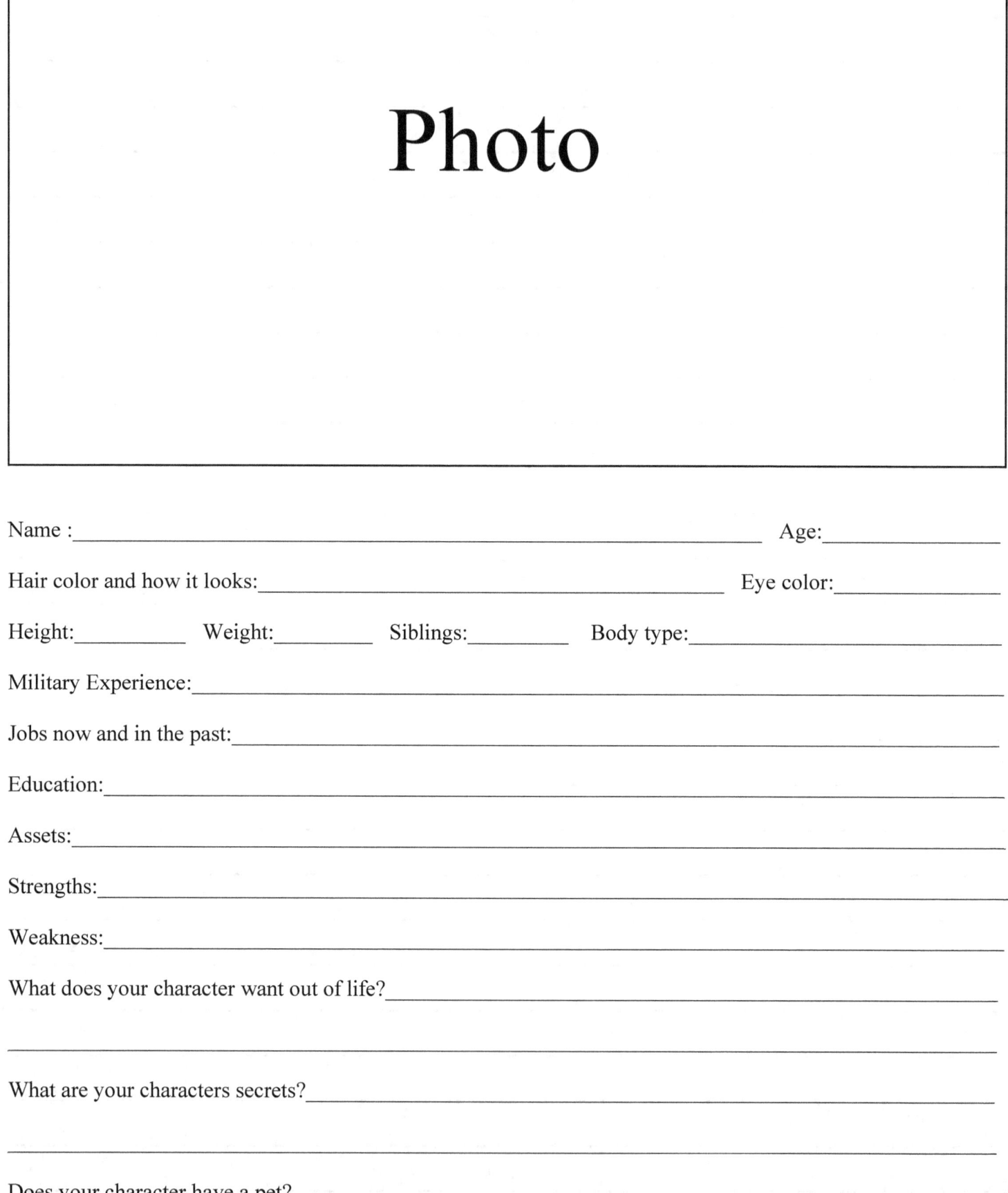

Photo

Name :_____ Age:_____

Hair color and how it looks:_____ Eye color:_____

Height:_____ Weight:_____ Siblings:_____ Body type:_____

Military Experience:_____

Jobs now and in the past:_____

Education:_____

Assets:_____

Strengths:_____

Weakness:_____

What does your character want out of life?_____

_____

What are your characters secrets?_____

_____

Does your character have a pet?_____

You get the idea. Have a conversion with your character and write it down.

Notes

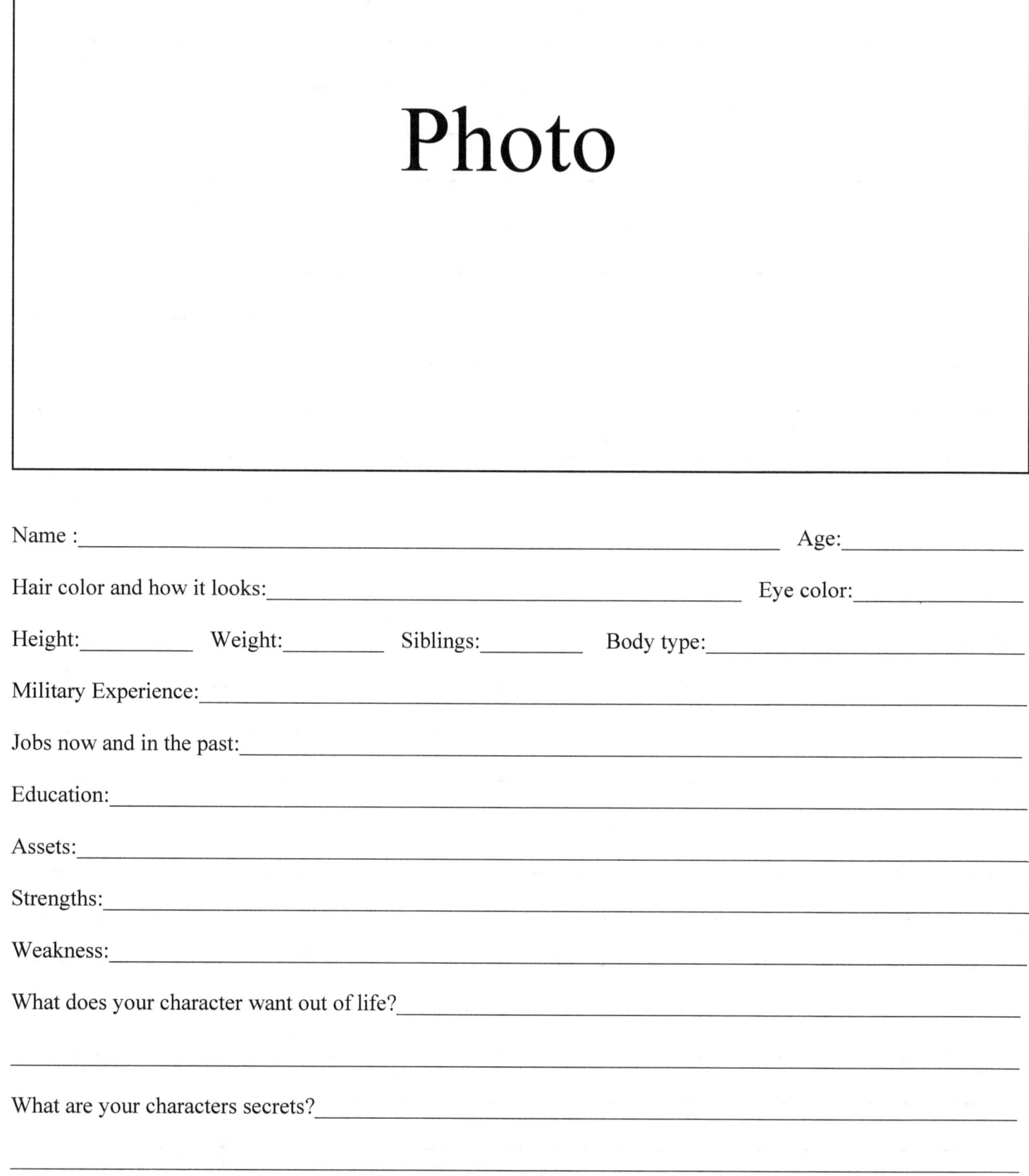

Name : _____ Age:_____

Hair color and how it looks:_____ Eye color:_____

Height:_____ Weight:_____ Siblings:_____ Body type:_____

Military Experience:_____

Jobs now and in the past:_____

Education:_____

Assets:_____

Strengths:_____

Weakness:_____

What does your character want out of life?_____

_____

What are your characters secrets?_____

_____

Does your character have a pet?_____

You get the idea. Have a conversion with your character and write it down.

Notes

Name :_____ Age:_____

Hair color and how it looks:_____ Eye color:_____

Height:_____ Weight:_____ Siblings:_____ Body type:_____

Military Experience:_____

Jobs now and in the past:_____

Education:_____

Assets:_____

Strengths:_____

Weakness:_____

What does your character want out of life?_____

_____

What are your characters secrets?_____

_____

Does your character have a pet?_____

You get the idea. Have a conversion with your character and write it down.

Notes

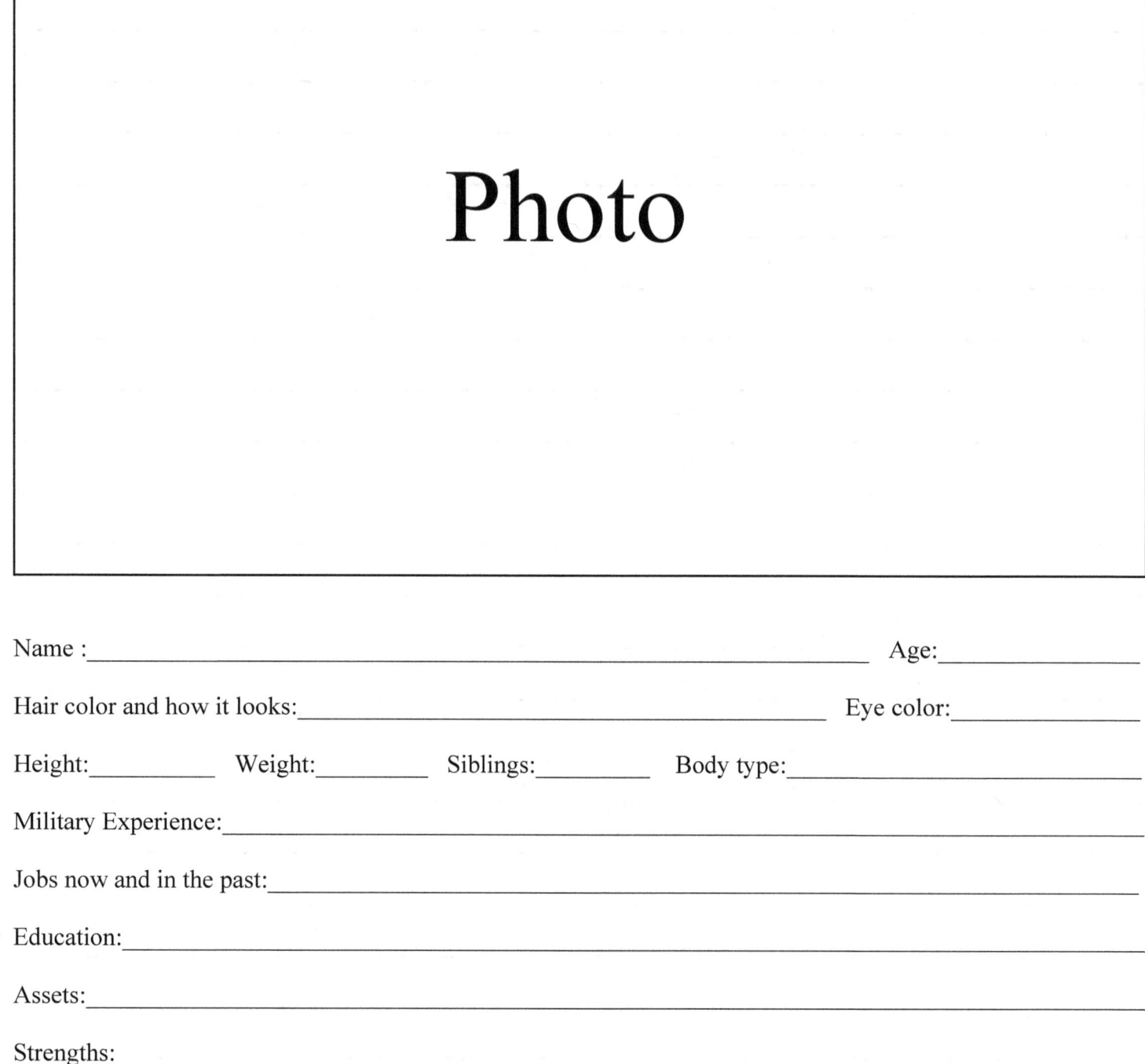

Photo

Name :_____ Age:_____

Hair color and how it looks:_____ Eye color:_____

Height:_____ Weight:_____ Siblings:_____ Body type:_____

Military Experience:_____

Jobs now and in the past:_____

Education:_____

Assets:_____

Strengths:_____

Weakness:_____

What does your character want out of life?_____

_____

What are your characters secrets?_____

_____

Does your character have a pet?_____

You get the idea. Have a conversion with your character and write it down.

Notes

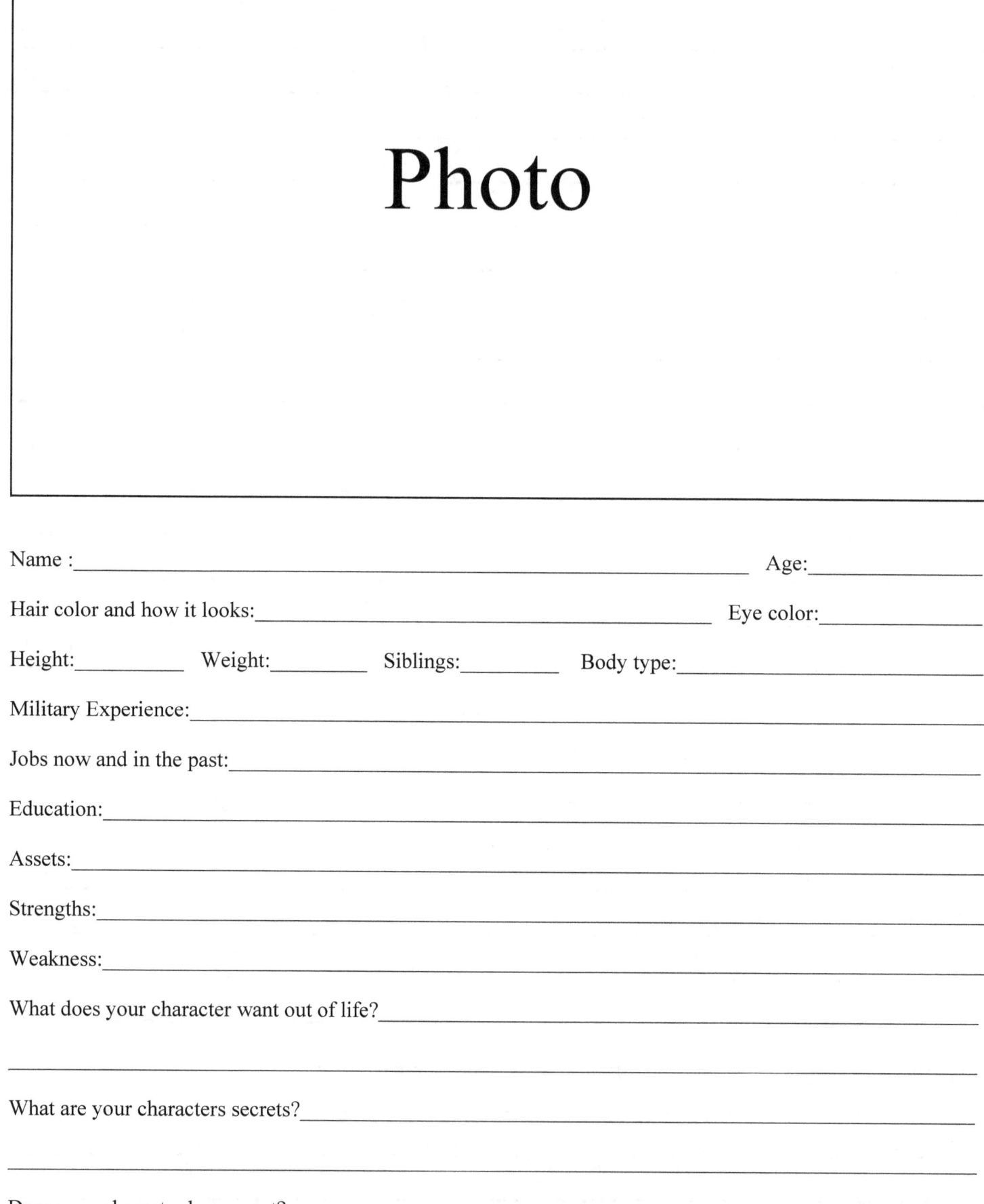

Photo

Name :_____ Age:_____

Hair color and how it looks:_____ Eye color:_____

Height:_____ Weight:_____ Siblings:_____ Body type:_____

Military Experience:_____

Jobs now and in the past:_____

Education:_____

Assets:_____

Strengths:_____

Weakness:_____

What does your character want out of life?_____

_____

What are your characters secrets?_____

_____

Does your character have a pet?_____

You get the idea. Have a conversion with your character and write it down.

Notes

Name :_____ Age:_____

Hair color and how it looks:_____ Eye color:_____

Height:_____ Weight:_____ Siblings:_____ Body type:_____

Military Experience:_____

Jobs now and in the past:_____

Education:_____

Assets:_____

Strengths:_____

Weakness:_____

What does your character want out of life?_____

_____

What are your characters secrets?_____

_____

Does your character have a pet?_____

You get the idea. Have a conversion with your character and write it down.

Notes

Name :_____ Age:_____

Hair color and how it looks:_____ Eye color:_____

Height:_____ Weight:_____ Siblings:_____ Body type:_____

Military Experience:_____

Jobs now and in the past:_____

Education:_____

Assets:_____

Strengths:_____

Weakness:_____

What does your character want out of life?_____

_____

What are your characters secrets?_____

_____

Does your character have a pet?_____

You get the idea. Have a conversion with your character and write it down.

Notes

Name :_____ Age:_____

Hair color and how it looks:_____ Eye color:_____

Height:_____   Weight:_____   Siblings:_____   Body type:_____

Military Experience:_____

Jobs now and in the past:_____

Education:_____

Assets:_____

Strengths:_____

Weakness:_____

What does your character want out of life?_____

_____

What are your characters secrets?_____

_____

Does your character have a pet?_____

You get the idea. Have a conversion with your character and write it down.

Notes

Photo

Name :_____ Age:_____

Hair color and how it looks:_____ Eye color:_____

Height:_____ Weight:_____ Siblings:_____ Body type:_____

Military Experience:_____

Jobs now and in the past:_____

Education:_____

Assets:_____

Strengths:_____

Weakness:_____

What does your character want out of life?_____

_____

What are your characters secrets?_____

_____

Does your character have a pet?_____

You get the idea. Have a conversion with your character and write it down.

Notes

Name :_____ Age:_____

Hair color and how it looks:_____ Eye color:_____

Height:_____ Weight:_____ Siblings:_____ Body type:_____

Military Experience:_____

Jobs now and in the past:_____

Education:_____

Assets:_____

Strengths:_____

Weakness:_____

What does your character want out of life?_____

_____

What are your characters secrets?_____

_____

Does your character have a pet?_____

You get the idea. Have a conversion with your character and write it down.

Notes

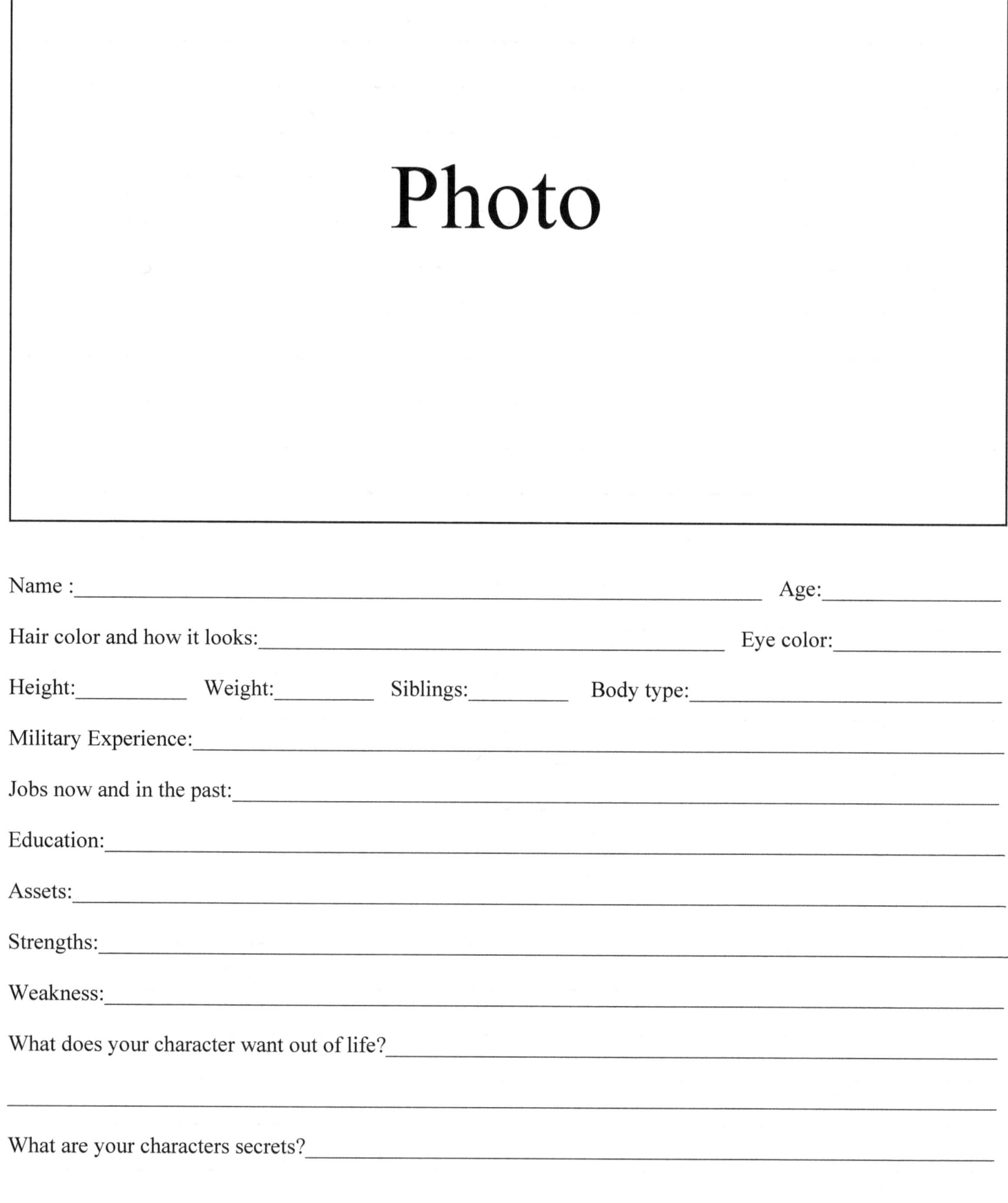

Photo

Name :_____ Age:_____

Hair color and how it looks:_____ Eye color:_____

Height:_____ Weight:_____ Siblings:_____ Body type:_____

Military Experience:_____

Jobs now and in the past:_____

Education:_____

Assets:_____

Strengths:_____

Weakness:_____

What does your character want out of life?_____

_____

What are your characters secrets?_____

_____

Does your character have a pet?_____

You get the idea. Have a conversion with your character and write it down.

Notes

Name :_____ Age:_____

Hair color and how it looks:_____ Eye color:_____

Height:_____ Weight:_____ Siblings:_____ Body type:_____

Military Experience:_____

Jobs now and in the past:_____

Education:_____

Assets:_____

Strengths:_____

Weakness:_____

What does your character want out of life?_____

_____

What are your characters secrets?_____

_____

Does your character have a pet?_____

You get the idea. Have a conversion with your character and write it down.

Notes

Name :_____ Age:_____

Hair color and how it looks:_____ Eye color:_____

Height:_____ Weight:_____ Siblings:_____ Body type:_____

Military Experience:_____

Jobs now and in the past:_____

Education:_____

Assets:_____

Strengths:_____

Weakness:_____

What does your character want out of life?_____

_____

What are your characters secrets?_____

_____

Does your character have a pet?_____

You get the idea. Have a conversion with your character and write it down.

Notes

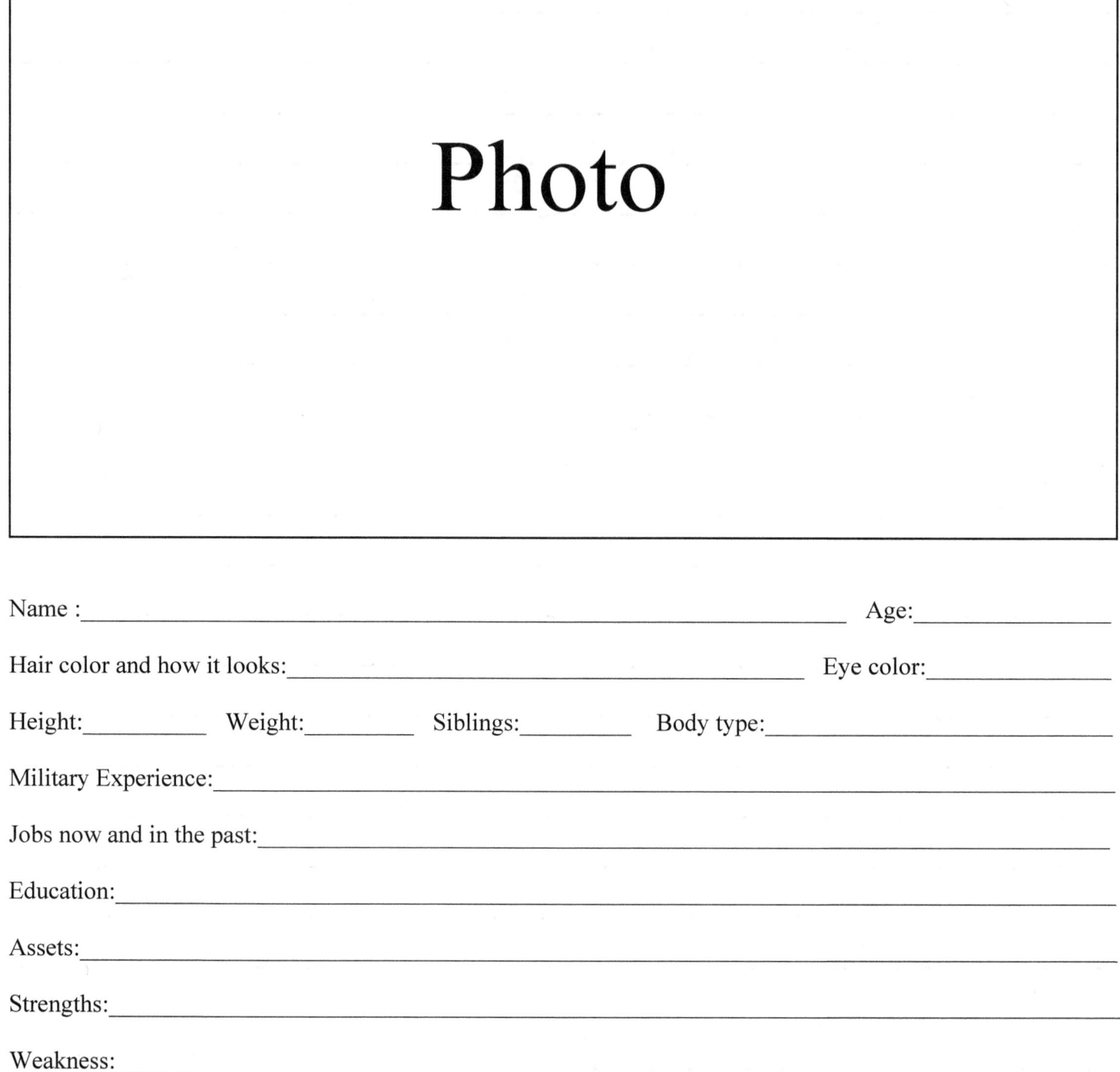

Photo

Name :_____ Age:_____

Hair color and how it looks:_____ Eye color:_____

Height:_____ Weight:_____ Siblings:_____ Body type:_____

Military Experience:_____

Jobs now and in the past:_____

Education:_____

Assets:_____

Strengths:_____

Weakness:_____

What does your character want out of life?_____

_____

What are your characters secrets?_____

_____

Does your character have a pet?_____

You get the idea. Have a conversion with your character and write it down.

Notes

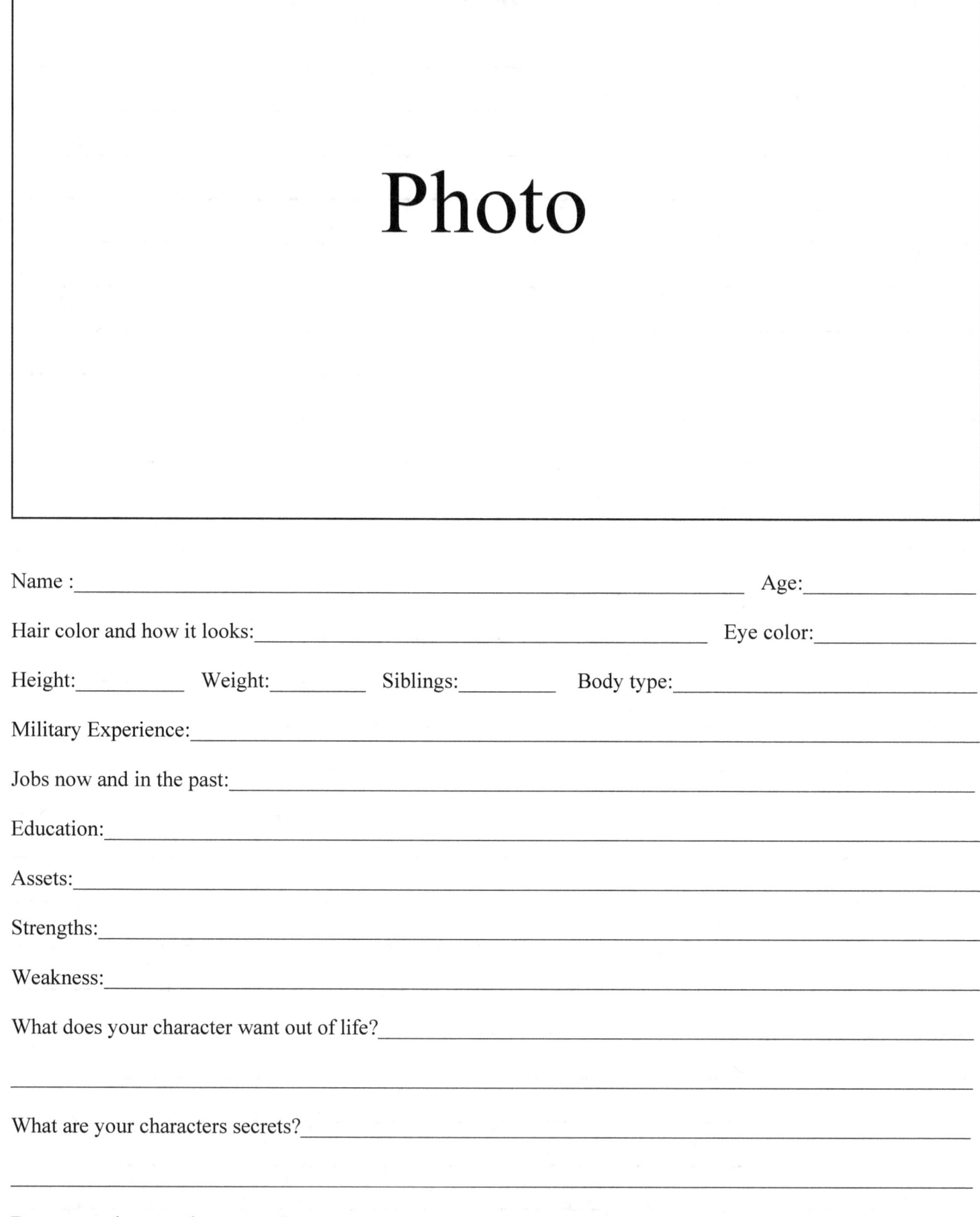

Name :_____ Age:_____

Hair color and how it looks:_____ Eye color:_____

Height:_____ Weight:_____ Siblings:_____ Body type:_____

Military Experience:_____

Jobs now and in the past:_____

Education:_____

Assets:_____

Strengths:_____

Weakness:_____

What does your character want out of life?_____

_____

What are your characters secrets?_____

_____

Does your character have a pet?_____

You get the idea. Have a conversion with your character and write it down.

Notes

Photo

Name :_____ Age:_____

Hair color and how it looks:_____ Eye color:_____

Height:_____ Weight:_____ Siblings:_____ Body type:_____

Military Experience:_____

Jobs now and in the past:_____

Education:_____

Assets:_____

Strengths:_____

Weakness:_____

What does your character want out of life?_____

_____

What are your characters secrets?_____

_____

Does your character have a pet?_____

You get the idea. Have a conversion with your character and write it down.

Notes

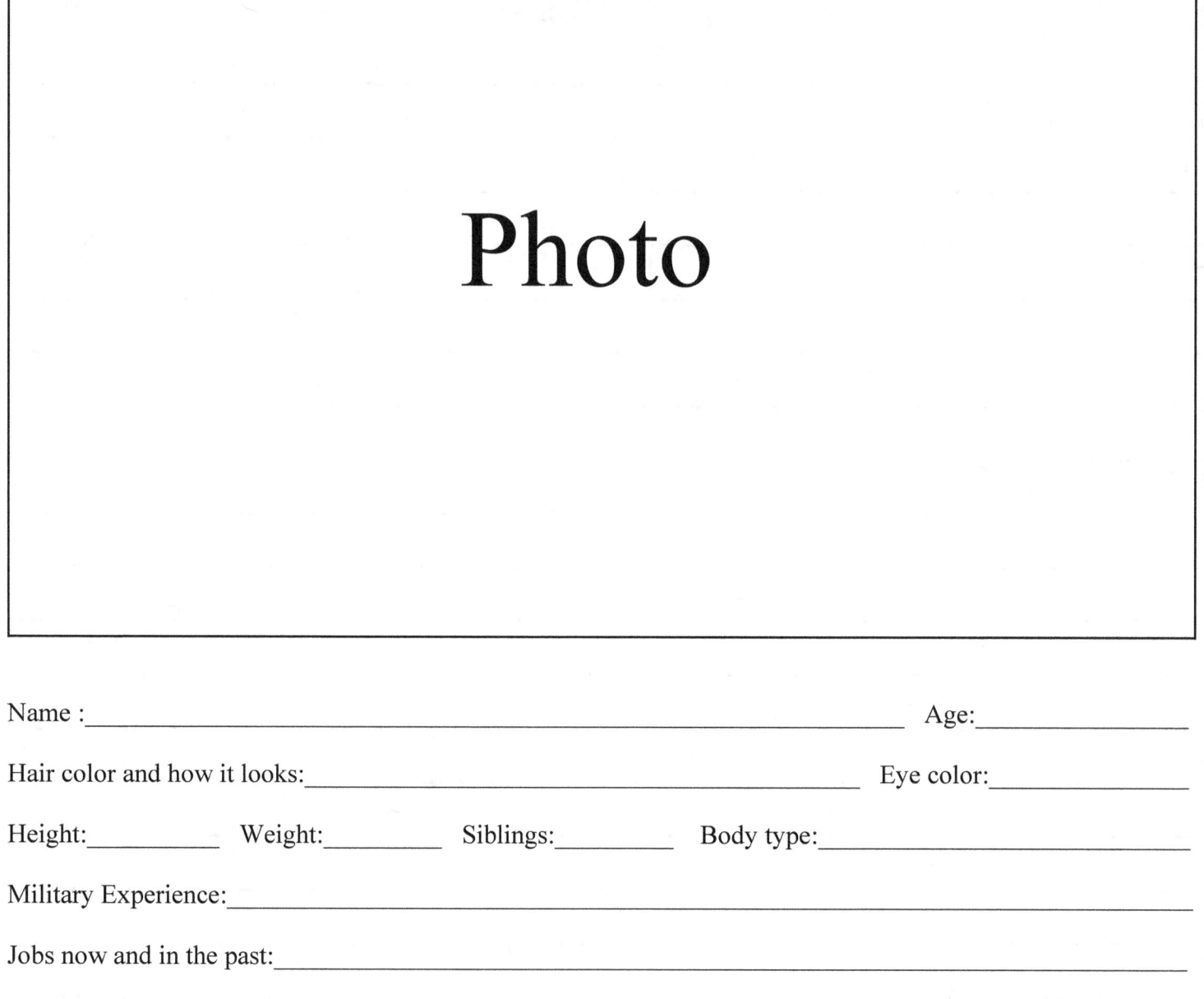

Name :_____ Age:_____

Hair color and how it looks:_____ Eye color:_____

Height:_____ Weight:_____ Siblings:_____ Body type:_____

Military Experience:_____

Jobs now and in the past:_____

Education:_____

Assets:_____

Strengths:_____

Weakness:_____

What does your character want out of life?_____

_____

What are your characters secrets?_____

_____

Does your character have a pet?_____

You get the idea. Have a conversion with your character and write it down.

Notes

Name :_____ Age:_____

Hair color and how it looks:_____ Eye color:_____

Height:_____ Weight:_____ Siblings:_____ Body type:_____

Military Experience:_____

Jobs now and in the past:_____

Education:_____

Assets:_____

Strengths:_____

Weakness:_____

What does your character want out of life?_____

_____

What are your characters secrets?_____

_____

Does your character have a pet?_____

You get the idea. Have a conversion with your character and write it down.

Notes

Photo

Name :_____ Age:_____

Hair color and how it looks:_____ Eye color:_____

Height:_____ Weight:_____ Siblings:_____ Body type:_____

Military Experience:_____

Jobs now and in the past:_____

Education:_____

Assets:_____

Strengths:_____

Weakness:_____

What does your character want out of life?_____

_____

What are your characters secrets?_____

_____

Does your character have a pet?_____

You get the idea. Have a conversion with your character and write it down.

Notes

Other Books you might like.

Relaxing Coloring Books for Adults
ISBN 13:978-1511781497
ISBN 10:1511781491

Relaxing Coloring Books for Adults Vol.2
ISBN 978-1514330395
ISBN 1514330393

These and other books can be found at Amazon, Barns & Noble and ordered at your favorite book store.

barbarappleby.weebly.com

Writer's Write Calendar And Organizer
Authored by Barbara Appleby

8.5" x 11" (21.59 x 27.94 cm)

Black & White on White paper

74 pages

ISBN-13: 978-1500943745 (CreateSpace-Assigned)

ISBN-10: 1500943746

BISAC: Language Arts & Disciplines / Publishing

"Writer's Write Calendar and Organizer" is a working writers best friend. It is a valuable tool to help make the most of their most precious resource; time. The handy planning calendar is useful to track projects, and increase your productivity and your income. This includes to Do List, Contacts Address, Notes, Book Launch, Editing Day, Password List, Blog Post Planner, Book Signings and Reservations. Make your planner a part of your life style and see the rewards of time well spent.

For sale on Amazon and can be order at all fine book stores

There are different covers for all calendars, receipt books, and journals
check out Amazon and your favorite book store.

List Price: **$9.97**

6" x 9" (15.24 x 22.86 cm)

Black & White on White paper

80 pages

ISBN-13: 978-1517323653 (CreateSpace-Assigned)

ISBN-10: 1517323657

BISAC: Business & Economics / Bookkeeping

A Writer's Write Receipt Book for author's to use at book signings

for book sells and preorders, will be an indie author's best friend.

There are 100 sets in each book and they are two part. One for the

book buyer that is cut off to take with them. The other stays in the

book for the year's end to prove to your self and the tax prepare

you are a selling author.

For sale on Amazon and can be order at all fine book stores

There are different covers for all calendars, receipt books, and journals
check out Amazon and your favorite book store.